MEL BAY'S

Finger Positions
for the Violin

BY TOM GILLAND

1 2 3 4 5 6 7 8 9 0

Visit us on the Web at www.melbay.com — E-mail us at email@melbay.com

The intention of this book is to illustrate where the fingers of the left hand are placed on the fingerboard of the violin.

The diagrams showing this are complemented by music notation. The $\wedge$ symbol between two notes shows that these two notes are only a semi-tone apart and the fingers on the fingerboard are therefore close together.

No attempt has been made to show the exact positions of the fingers on the fingerboard since this depends on several factors. What is shown is where two fingers are either close together, as for a semi-tone, or further apart, as for a tone.

Only the first four positions are illustrated as after this the fifth position has the same relative finger positions as the first position, the sixth the same as the second and so on.

To position the hand for the second position first of all place the hand for the first position. Then move the hand until the first finger is where the second finger was. You are now in the second position.

For the third position move the hand from the first position until the first finger is where the third finger was. To get to the fourth position first of all move the hand from the first to the third position and then move the first finger until it is where the second finger was in the third position.

This book is dedicated to my wife Anice, who is a long suffering 'fiddle widow,' to my parents Betty and Alex Gilland and last, but not least, to my violin teacher Alex J. Lawson.

Table of Contents

Third Position

Fourth Position

First Position

C Major ✓

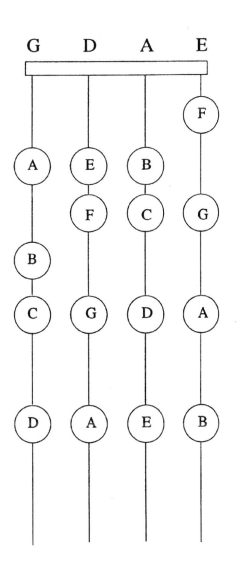

First Position

G Major

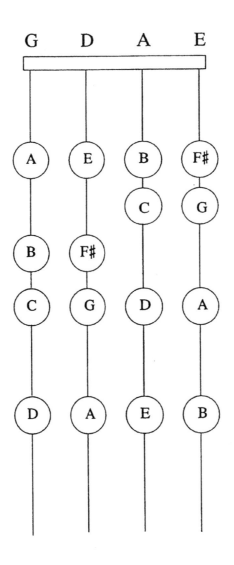

First Position

D Major

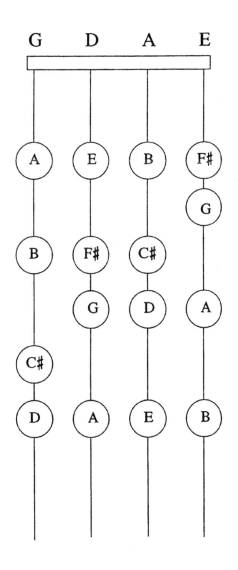

First Position

A Major

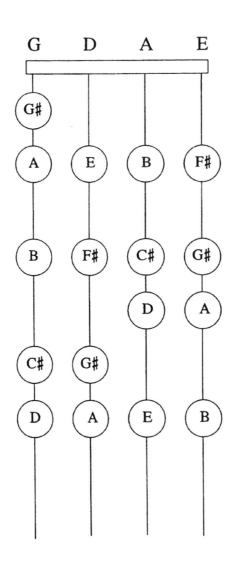

First Position

E Major

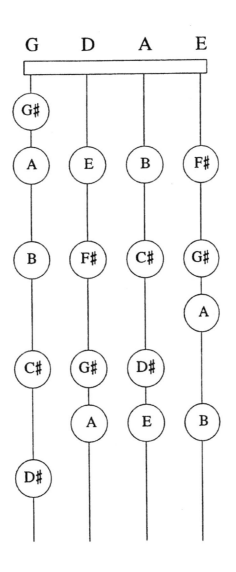

First Position

B Major

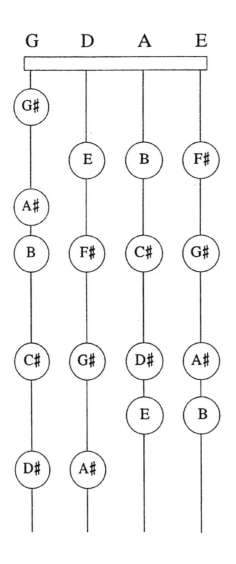

First Position

F♯ Major

F#C#G#D#A#E#

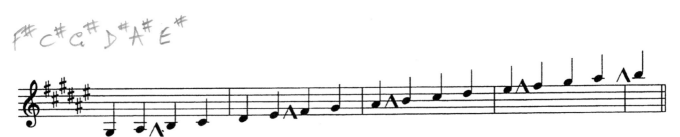

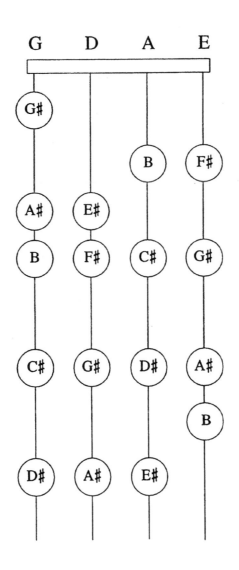

First Position

F Major

Bb.

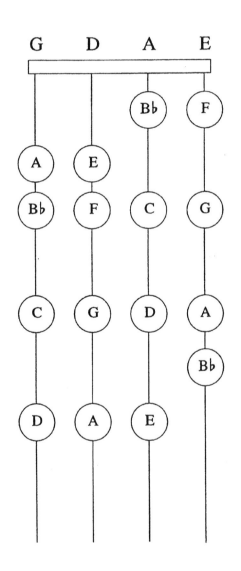

First Position

B♭ Major

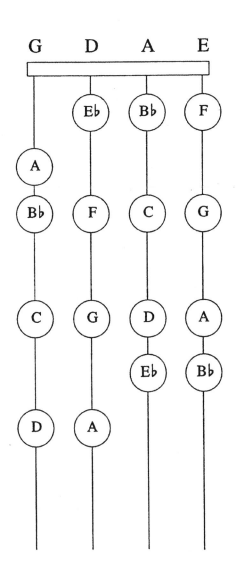

13

First Position

E♭ Major

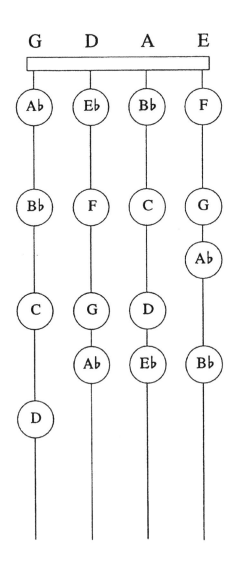

First Position

A♭ Major

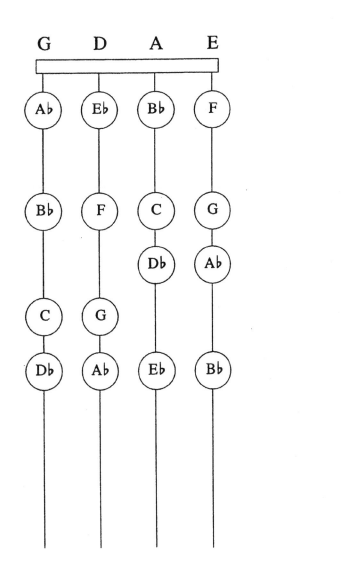

First Position

D♭ Major

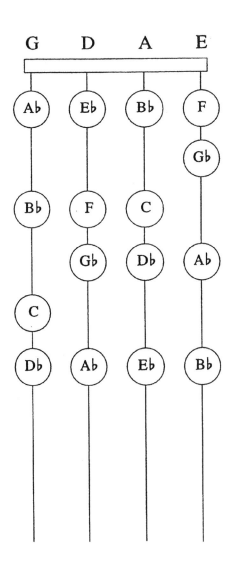

First Position

G♭ Major

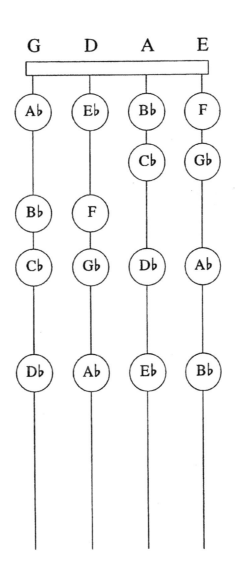

Second Position

C Major

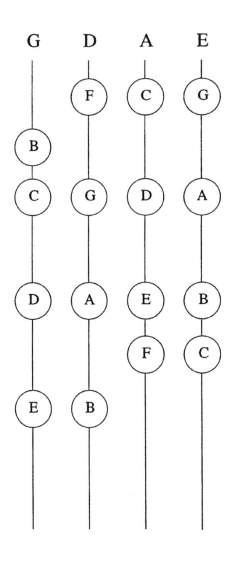

Second Position

G Major

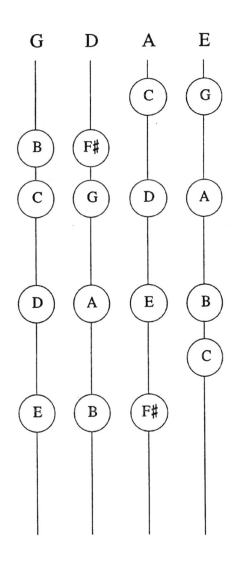

Second Position

D Major

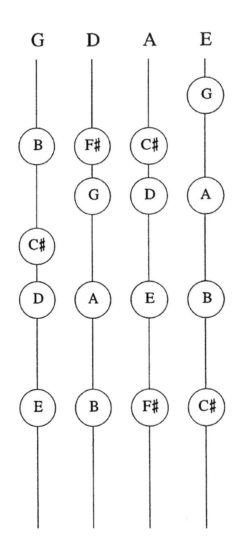

Second Position

A Major

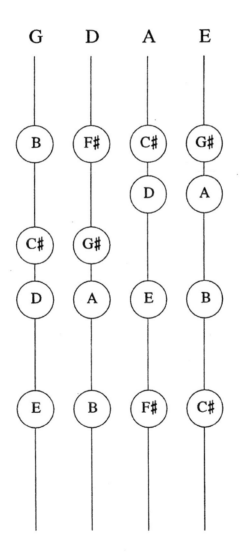

Second Position

E Major

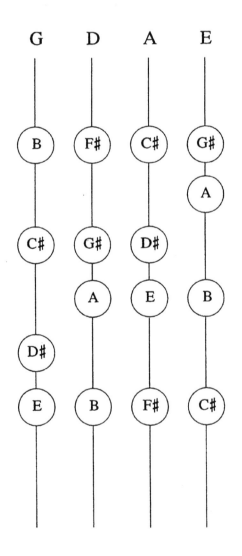

Second Position

B Major

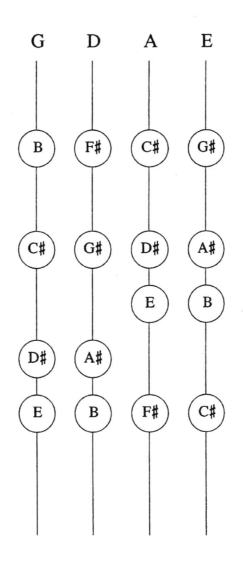

Second Position

F# Major

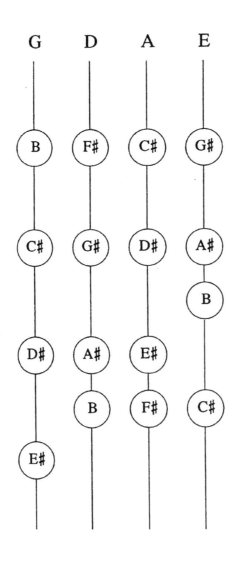

Second Position

F Major

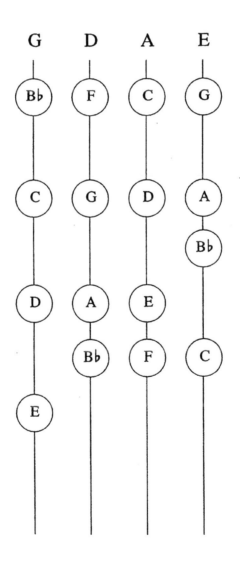

Second Position

B♭ Major

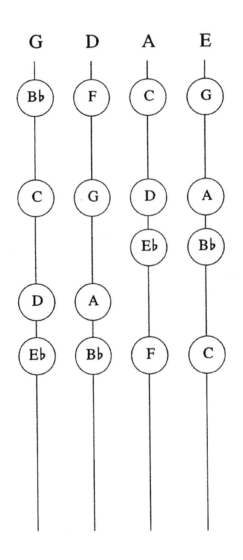

26

Second Position

E♭ Major

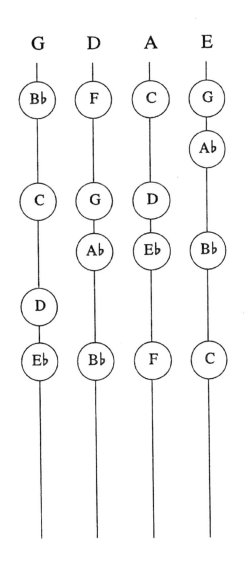

Second Position

A♭ Major

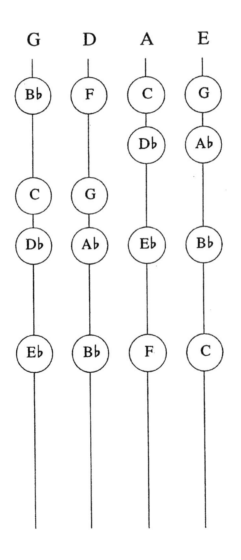

Second Position

D♭ Major

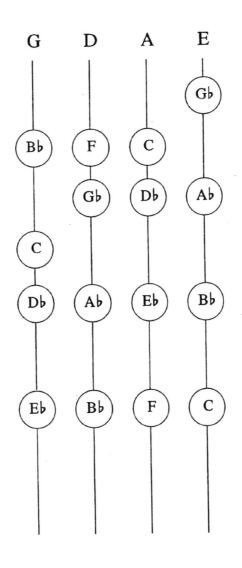

Second Position

G♭ Major

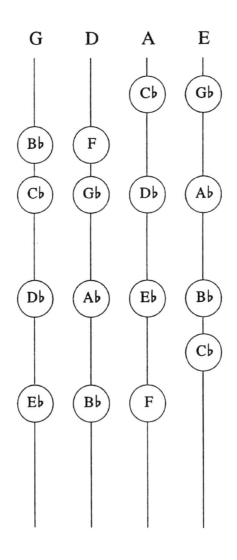

Third Position

C Major

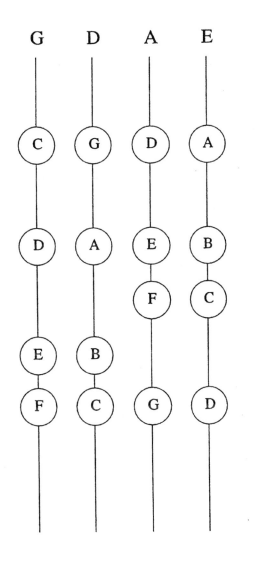

Third Position

G Major

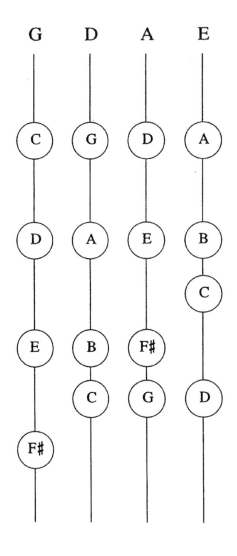

Third Position

D Major

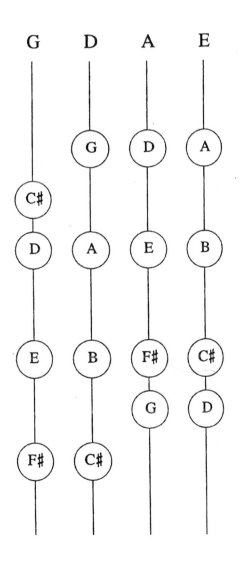

Third Position

A Major

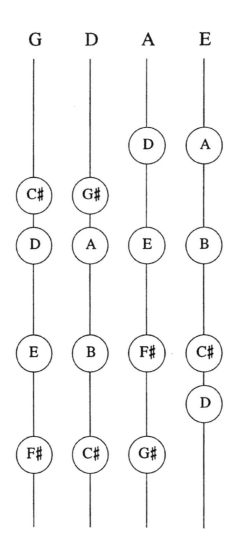

Third Position

E Major

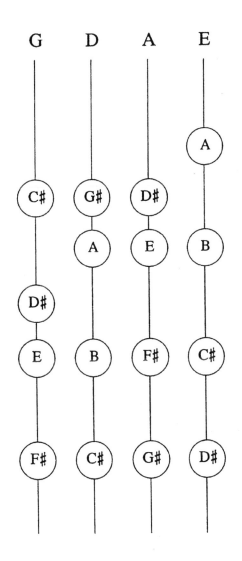

Third Position

B Major

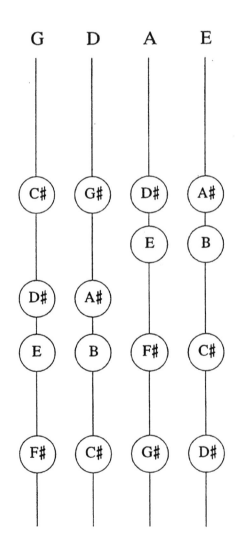

Third Position

F♯ Major

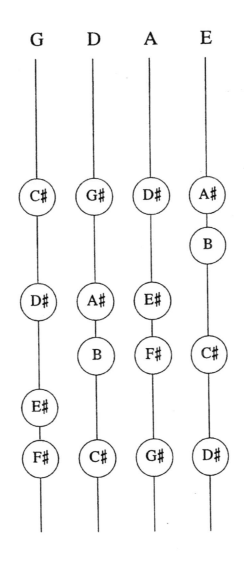

Third Position

F Major

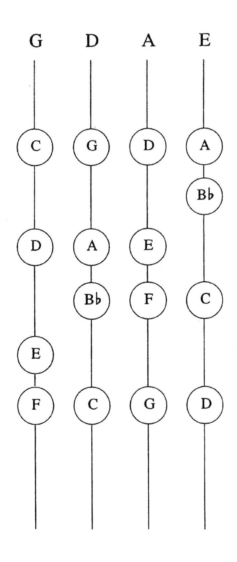

Third Position

B♭ Major

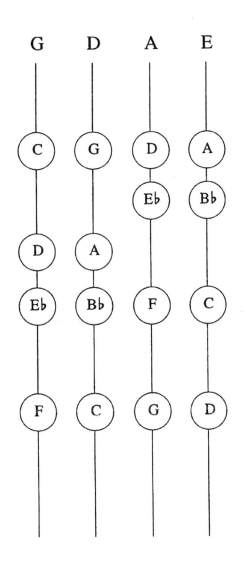

Third Position

E♭ Major

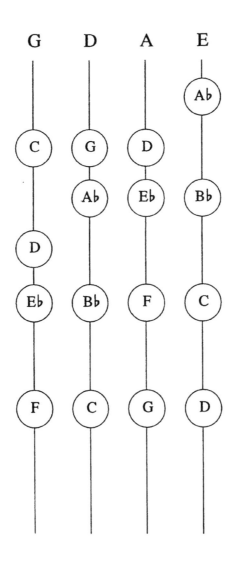

Third Position

A♭ Major

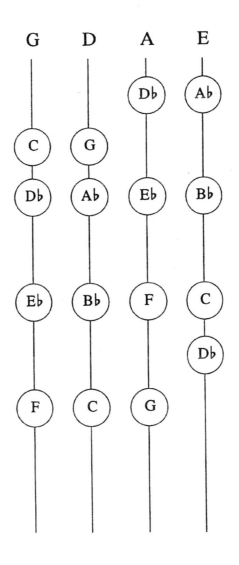

Third Position

D♭ Major

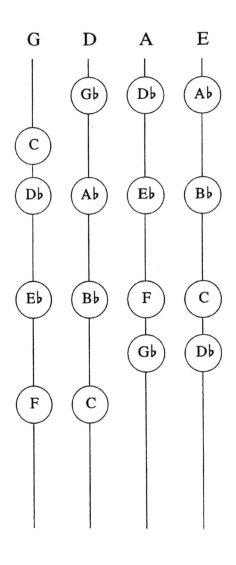

Third Position

G♭ Major

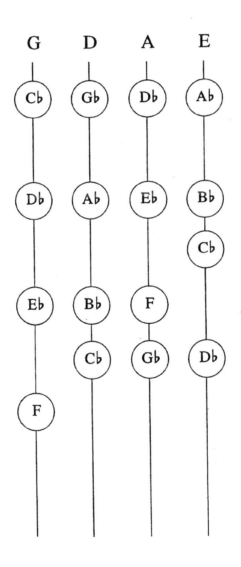

43

Fourth Position

C Major

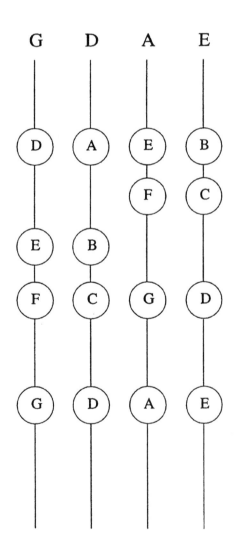

Fourth Position

G Major

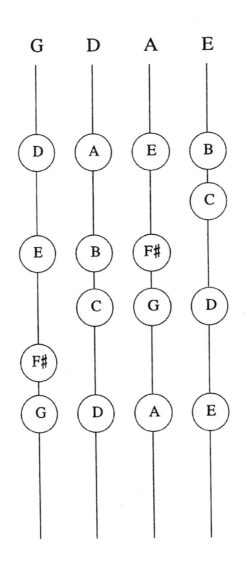

Fourth Position

D Major

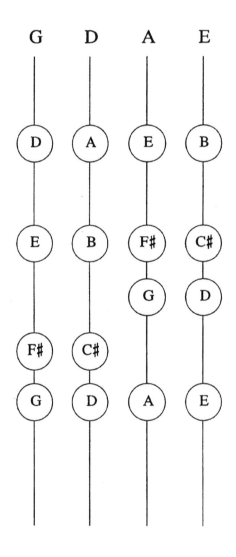

Fourth Position

A Major

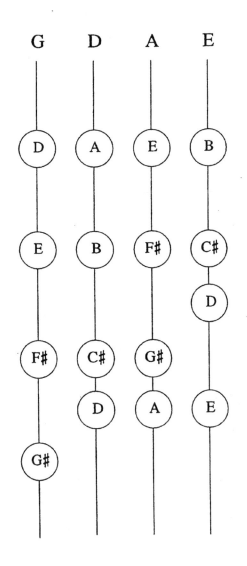

Fourth Position

E Major

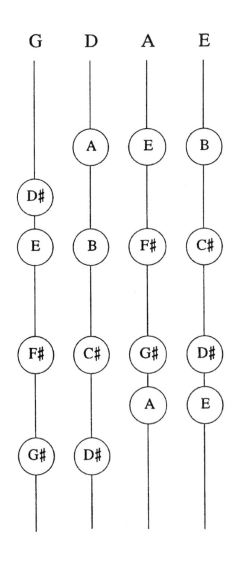

Fourth Position

B Major

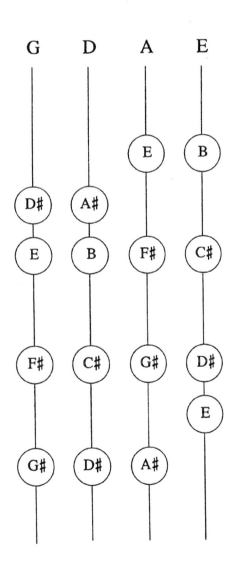

Fourth Position

F# Major

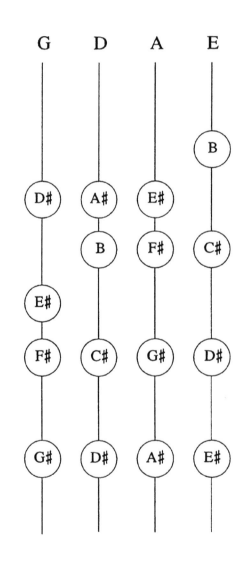

Fourth Position

F Major

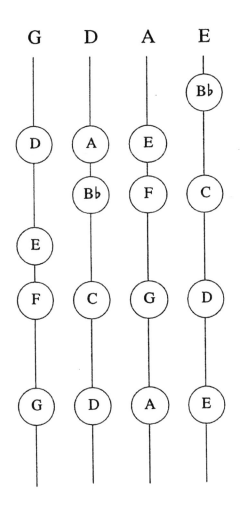

Fourth Position

B♭ Major

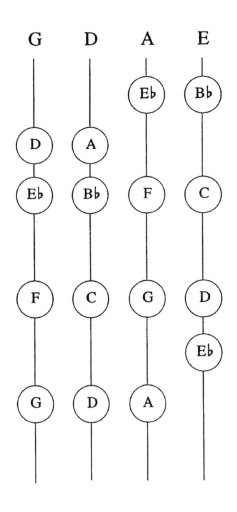

Fourth Position

E♭ Major

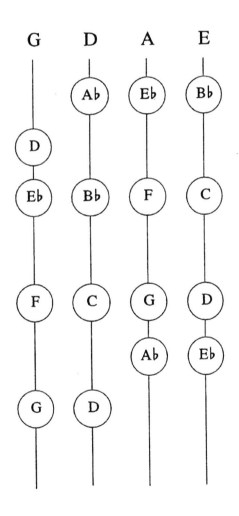

Fourth Position

A♭ Major

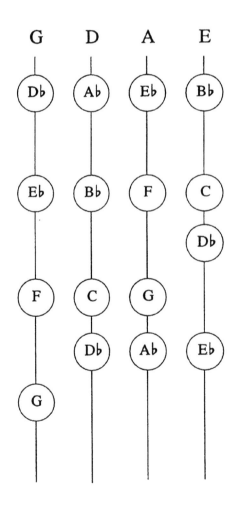

Fourth Position

Db Major

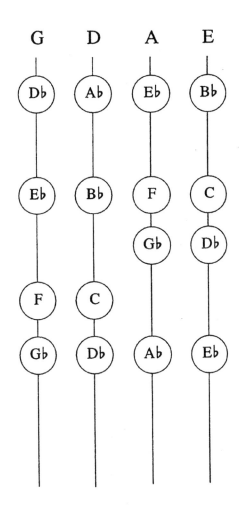

Fourth Position

G♭ Major

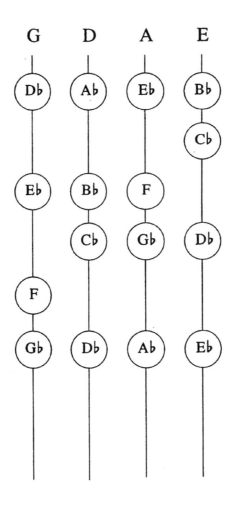

Printed in Great Britain
by Amazon